Copyright 2019 Cassandra Allen
All rights reserved
Published by Cassandra Allen/Lulu Press, Inc.
627 Davis Drive, Suite 300, Morrisville, NC 27560

Scripture quotations marked KJV are from the Holy Bible, King James Version
(Authorized Version) First published in 1611, Quoted from The KJV Classic Copyright Reference Bible,
Copyright 1983 by Zondervan Corporation

Scripture quotations marked NLT are taken from the Holy Bible, New Living Translation,
Copyright 1996, 2004 and 2007

ISBN 978-0-578-59253-4

DEDICATION

Thank you, Kaden Isaiah Hargrove, for encouraging me. You probably don't even realize the role you played in keeping me accountable to finish this book. I remember the day you asked me the name of the book. From that day on, almost every time you saw me, you asked if I had written it yet. I knew I had to finish it because I want to set a good example for you in your life. Always be a finisher in everything you do. If you don't quit, you'll always be a winner.

Leslie Hargrove, thank you for being such an amazing son. I thank God for you. You're quiet, kind and giving. You're a blessing to everyone who meets you. Thank you for being understand and forgiving not only with me but with others too. You are a man of God with strong character and endurance.

Finally thank you Terry Peak, Jr. you are amazing. For a while it was just the two of us, so you've always been my best friend. You too are a mighty man of God. There hasn't been a time in my life that I couldn't count on you. Thanks for listening and being honest. You have given so much to so many and you never even ask for anything in return. Your heart is pure and if anyone can't see it, shame on them. You've faced many obstacles but know that you will have the victory.

The three of you are my family and closer to me than anyone else. I love you all to life. Nothing will ever separate us.

INTRODUCTION

All my life I've been disappointed and hurt. I've always expected it to happen again. I taught myself not to trust anyone. I took what people said with a grain of salt. I'd been lied to so many times. People were always saying one thing but doing another. I couldn't trust anybody.

I've learned to live with a wall of protection around me. I was certain it would shield me from rejection. But it didn't stop the pain and disappointment. I had failed yet again. I tried to control my expectations of others to avoid being hurt by them. The horrible thing about that is unknowingly I included God. He would never hurt me. He loves me and only wants to help me. God is a gentleman and will not force his way into my life. He looks at my heart. He knows how much I want and need him. He will walk me through the process of healing. He will destroy the wall that separates us. I must let God in to receive his promises and blessings.

Not only did I shield myself, I included my children too. I didn't want them to experience the same pain. By protecting them, I caused damage to their lives too. My children were being rejected just as I was. I would protect them even from my own family members. My family has literally been torn into pieces. It's not a curse because we're no longer under the curse of the law but under the blessing. It must be a stronghold in my family. I pray for God to send my children godly wives and families. I want them to know what families are really like. I pray the same prayer for myself and my grandson. I know God has heard my prayers. It's not God's will for families to be torn apart.

My grandson is seven years old and my mom had seven siblings. He has many cousins, but he doesn't know any of them. He never has an opportunity to spend time with any of them. This saddens me because he wants to see them, but I can't seem to make it happen. I try reaching out, but no one responds. I pray that God fills his life and surrounds him with loving family members.

I wait for God to turn around the lives of my children as well as my own. I used to blame myself for the things I did around them. But now I wait for God's promise that my seed is blessed. I wait to see the manifestation of this promise in my life. I'm excited for the day that I am in church with my entire family worshiping God. Thank you, Lord. We will walk in the blessing of the Lord. They shall know the truth and the truth shall make them free.

STRUGGLES

    I have an obstacle in front of me called food. I am very discouraged about my weight. It seems that I'm gaining weight every day. It's not comfortable moving around and doing things when I'm so heavy. I can't seem to get the pounds off no matter what. About five years ago, I decided to exercise and eat right. I wanted to lose weight and get fit. I began by walking every day and making changes in my diet. I eventually joined a health club and worked out a few days a week. At one point, I realized that I was close to obsessing over it. I was going to the gym way too much. At first, I was self-conscious and didn't really concentrate on my fitness goals. I got on the treadmill and that was about it. Then I was introduced to a three- day diet. I tried it more than once and it was horrible. I was literally starving myself. I went three days eating a little of nothing. It was not a realistic plan. I've exercised for years now with no results. I was desperate to lose the weight so I would try just about anything. There was a ten-day cleanse that I also tried several times. During that time, I drank fruit and veggie smoothies. When I wanted something to chew, it was raw veggies. I shed pounds each time but gained them all back. I joined one health club after another, and I wasn't losing any weight. Finally, I signed up for a weight loss program and the pounds started coming off very nicely. I did it for about six months and lost just over 30 pounds. Then I went on vacation and we ate out every single day and sometimes twice a day. I put a few pounds back on, but I still looked and felt great.

One day I picked my grandson up from school and took him out to eat. This should not have been a problem, but I was deceived. I ordered corn and green beans. Suddenly, I heard a voice remind me that potatoes are a vegetable too. I wondered why I'd been deprived myself of potatoes. Afterall potatoes are a vegetable. I ordered fries and for the next month I ate them every day. I gained all the weight back and then some. I can't seem to stop eating some days. This was five years ago, and I have not conquered this yet. I'm bigger now than I ever was and I'm afraid of getting bigger still. Sometimes I cry because I don't understand how this can be happening. God delivered me from addiction so what's the problem? When I talk to people about this, they offer me advice on how to eat. What time to stop eating and the importance of exercising. If they only knew how long I've dealt with this.

Helpful people suggest that I change my eating habits. I've tried that but I'm still overeating. I don't know how to stop on my own. I cry out to God and ask him to take away the desire to overeat. My oldest son is the same way. He eats even when he's full. I don't understand why? Some call it comfort food but it's very uncomfortable to be stuffed. At first, I thought my son had an addiction to food but that can't be true. That would mean I still had the spirit of addiction. I know for a fact that God delivered me from that spirit. I must hear God in this area so that we will be set free. I know it's an evil spirit's operation, but I don't know what. I think about the number of years I was in addiction and I don't want the same for my son. I want him to have the blessed life that God promises us.

So now, here I am with a mountain in front of me. Interfering with my relationship with my

Father. I must do something about it because I must keep moving forward. I will continue to draw closer to my God. They don't understand how difficult this is for me. Now I'm abusing food. What seems so simple to some can seem impossible to others. **Mark 11:23,(NKJV) says *"For assuredly, I say to you whoever says to this mountain, "Be removed and be cast into the sea," and does not doubt in his heart, but believes that those things he says will be done, he will have whatever he says.***

I get tired of trying but I won't quit. People all around me are losing weight and getting healthy. I don't know why I haven't done it yet. When will I ever get this right? I'm uncomfortable sleeping at night. I'm squeezing into clothes that don't fit. They're too tight and the zippers are coming down constantly. The worst part of it is that it looks terrible. I pray all the time and ask God to help me, but he hasn't yet. Or should I say it's already done, and I just don't see the results yet? I know God will help me he's done it in the past. I pray God's word to him because he says don't worry about what to wear. I don't know what to do. I look at people around me and no one seems to be in this battle except me. I know that's not true but nevertheless, it feels that way. I try not to focus on it, but I still find myself thinking about it. When I look in the mirror, I look for changes in my body and I see them. I only wish they were positive changes. I just don't understand. I try everything to stop eating so much but nothing changes. There must be a reason for this, and I ask God to show me what it is. I'm so tired and I don't know what to do except wait on God. Instead of getting smaller I'm getting bigger every day. Again, I ask myself why me? I know God loves me and he is faithful. But why do I have to stay in things so long?

    I get plenty of sleep every night. But when I wake up, I'm sleepy again within a couple of hours. There are no overweight people in my immediate circle other than me. Everyone else is losing weight so why can't I. Lord haven't I gone through enough? I've been so faithful Lord. I pray more, I read the bible more, and I watch the words that come out of my mouth. I treat people better than I ever have and yet I still feel stuck.

Once I heard God whisper to me that food has no power over me. If that's true, why can't I stop over- eating. There must be something else going on inside of me. I know that God is working it all out. He did it once with the drugs and tobacco and God is the same. So, I'm waiting to lose weight.

It seems like I'm waiting on everything but it's in the Lord's hands. I haven't given up. I'll never give up because God will never give up on me. Today a lady told me how much weight I gained, and I recently lost five pounds. This lady was addicted to crack cocaine. My first thought was to remind her of her own imperfections. But I decided not to respond to her carelessness. I thank God that he has changed me.

In a vision God showed me a saucer of food. I thought meant I should eat smaller portions to lose the weight. I ate from a saucer a few times and then went back to my old ways. I was determined to be successful, so I went to the store and bought portion-controlled plates. I have yet to use them. I prayed and asked God to help me to eat less food. I asked him to show me why this was happening. Food was winning the battle over my health. Sometimes the enemy tells me that I shouldn't ask God for simple things. But if I don't ask him, who will I ask? He is a present help in times of trouble. I can cast my burdens upon him, and He shall sustain me. He is the same God who delivered me from addiction, and he changes not. Faith is the substance of things hoped for and the evidence of things not seen. I do have faith that this will all change one day. I only wish I knew when. He's always with me and he hears my prayers when I pray according to His will. God said when I delight myself in him, He'll give me the desires of my heart. I truly desire to lose weight and I will.

Recently, I called one of my sister's in Christ and told her how I constantly eat. I confessed that I eat even when I'm already full. She is physically fit, exercises regularly and a healthy eater. I asked her if she would help me in any way she could. I didn't tell her that food was tormenting me. I told her I had been praying and asking God for his help. I told her how miserable I felt because of the extra weight I was carrying around. I shared that this reminds me of drug addiction. The spirit of addiction was no longer in me, or was it? It seemed so simple, just stop eating but it wasn't simple for me. I also told her that I thought I was an emotional eater. She began to speak, and I listened very carefully to what she had to say. Bluntly she said my body was an area God would not fix for me. She talked about the necessity of exercise and a healthy diet. She also stated that the body requires adequate rest. She reminded me that God gave dominion to man. The Greater One lives inside me. I must submit to God through His word; resist the devil and he will flee.

    The Holy Spirit reminded that I have authority over the power of the enemy. Instead of crying about it, I needed to remove the mountain it and cast it into the sea. It was then that a light bulb turned on in my mind. I was ready to take authority over this situation. I had a new strength and a new attitude about it. That night I turned on the television to find some biblical teaching. I listened to the teaching and she was talking directly to me. She said getting things from God may be uncomfortable for a while, but it gets easier. She used the example of someone wanting to lose weight as an illustration. I thought, finally I understand what to do. I was certain that I was in control and ready for battle. I would surely meet and exceed my weight loss goals. But here I am two years, three, four, five years later and haven't met them yet. God created me and knows me better than I know myself. Doesn't he realized that I can't do it without him. I may be waiting for God's help. But there must be something He's waiting for me to do.

I've been praying to God for quite some time now for clothes to wear. I've bought clothes, lost weight and gave them away. Now I've gained weight and I have almost nothing to wear. ***Matthew 6:31 says, so don't worry, saying "What shall we eat?" or "What shall we drink?" or "What shall we wear?" Matthew 6:32 says for pagans run after all these things, and your heavenly Father knows that you need them. Matthew 6:33 but seek first His kingdom and His righteousness, and all these things will be given to you as well.*** I pray, I believe, and I cry but I'll never give up on God. I won't doubt His word.

I didn't wait instead I went out and used my charge card to buy a couple of items. I had been wearing the same pants for a week at a time. I had to do something because now there was a hole in the pants. God knew this because He knows everything. I ask myself what I did wrong. This is a promise from God, and I seek Him daily, so I don't understand. This charge card had a zero balance for quite a while. Now in one week I used it for my grandson and myself. How would I pay this bill? I was already struggling to pay all my other bills. In addition to that I only have $2.00 in my wallet and my gas hand is on empty. I'm a tither and a giver so what am I waiting for? I still have faith in God because of all He's done for me. I know how much He loves me and His plan to prosper me. All I can do is to keep walking and keep trusting Him. He didn't leave me when I was living a life of sin. He surely won't leave me now.

I'm learning scriptures and I thought I was applying them to my life. I repeat them because I want them in my heart. I must be consistent. I have to say what God says and fight the good fight of faith. This isn't just for money or material things. This is so I can keep walking into my destiny. If there is anything in my way, it would only be two things. It's either myself or the enemy and I must communicate with God. He will lead me along the way I should go. The enemy must go because he is already defeated. God has given me authority over the enemy. There are angels fighting for me. Jesus is seated on the right hand of the Father, interceding on my behalf. I win every time. No weapon formed against me shall prosper unless I allow it to. The word is my weapon along with the blood and the name Jesus. These three things will always lead to victory.

    I may be delivered from addiction but I'm clueless to God's nature. I know nothing about his word or his will. I thought all things would fall into place but that's not God's way. It's a journey in which I'm learning and growing in the Lord. The enemy tosses me back and forth like a rag doll. He held me captive in condemnation. I thought I didn't deserve anything from God because of my past. I was convinced to stop waiting because HE wouldn't do it for me anyway. But he'll do anything I ask that lines up with his word. When I believe it in my heart and don't doubt it in my mind, I've already received it. I was treating him like a man instead of God. Forgive me Father and I repent of that sin right now. I plead the blood of Jesus over my heart and mind. Wash me and cleanse me Father and make me whole. Heal my heart and mind of all the brokenness and lies that have been planted there. I will see the goodness of the Lord in the land of the living. I will see your promises manifest in my life. I will see my children's lives changed. Thank you, Jesus, my Lord, my Redeemer. We will worship you as a family in spirit and in truth.

    I used to go to different people for advice about my life. This was so confusing because everyone said something different. They tried to help without having the solutions to my problems. I didn't trust myself or the relationship I had with God. Instead I trusted in what others were telling me. Until one day I finally got the revelation to put God first. He created me and he knows my purpose. I began to go to God and ask him questions.   I didn't think He was answering me. Sometimes other people told me things that God said. I was hurt that He spoke to them instead of telling me. I was so confused and afraid that I would mess up again. I wouldn't even go to my pastors. I thought God didn't want me talking to anyone except Him. I was trying so hard to get it right. Honestly, I think I was trying too hard. I needed to get out of the way and let God take care of things. All of this was happening because I didn't know the word. I had to spend more time with God, or I would never know him. I had to know more about him. I had to stop thinking and worry about things of this world. I had to change the way I was praying. I couldn't always ask God to do something for me. I began to pray and ask God what I could do for Him. This made a huge difference. He began speaking to my spirit and I could hear Him. He was showing me what would happen before it happened. Most of the things He showed me didn't happen right away. Sometimes I felt like God was giving me pieces to a puzzle. I will keep believing what God shows me and it will come to past.

Sometimes I find myself thinking about the things I want. Then I'm reminded my life doesn't belong to me. God says to seek ye first the kingdom of God and his righteousness. He knows what I need before I do, and He provides. God doesn't hold my past over my head for the rest of my life. He says to put him in remembrance of His word, not my past. This is one of the reasons I love Him so much.   He helps me along the way with whatever I need. When I confess my sins, He is faithful and just to forgive my sins and cleanse me of all unrighteousness.

   Obedience is better than sacrifice and everything in me wants to be obedient to God. There are times that I'm disobedient, but I must keep going. I don't do it on purpose, but it happens. God has been talking to me for quite a while now. I hear him sometimes, but I want to talk to him daily.   I shouldn't be confused about whether it's really Him speaking to me. However, sometimes I'm not sure of the identity of the voice I hear. I've been told there are three voices; God's, mine and the enemies. At times I get frustrated because I'm uncertain of who I'm hearing. Then I panic even more because God says, "my sheep know my voice." Does this mean I don't belong to God? Of course not, I belong to him. Lord help me because I need you every second of every day. Sometimes God tells me to do things and I miss it. This saddens me so much because I want to please God.

I was walking in the mall one day with my sister and there was a man standing alone. We walked past him, and something told me to go back. I asked the man if he was alright and he said yes. He said he only needed to catch his breath. I turned and walked away in the direction where my sister was standing. I looked back at the man as I continued walking away. I was so unsettled inside something wasn't right about this. I looked back at him again and yet I still walked away. I believe my spirit speaking to me. But at the same time, I believe the enemy was speaking to me too. The enemy was telling me, it would be foolish for me to go back. I didn't go and I regretted it for the rest of the night. I should have prayed with him, laid my hand on him and waited with him until he was better. Instead I left him all alone while he was having trouble breathing. Later, I told my sister that I should have gone back. I shared with her how bad I felt because I didn't. It was guilt and condemnation that I was feeling. I felt like a complete failure. I didn't think I would ever get it right. There is no condemnation for those who are in Christ Jesus. When you love someone as much as I love God, you always want to please them. But the enemy was constantly reminding me that once again I missed it. Together my sister and I prayed and asked God to forgive us and to heal the man. I know and understand the importance of doing what God tells me to do when He tells me to do it. I can't pick and choose because it's not my way, it's God's way. I always want to please my Father.

   I wake up every day praying and asking God to strengthen me for what I will face. There seems to be turmoil all around me. People are going through so much. My family situation is still not what I would like it to be. I must accept it for what is and keep moving forward. I don't look the way I want to look. I don't have the things I would like to have. Every time I take one step forward; I fall back ten. It seems like I'll never get ahead or even catch up for that matter. I'll never stop seeking God because he is faithful.

   God always seems to bless me when I least expect it. Yesterday a lady from church told me God instructed her to bless me with $100.00. We were at the doctor's office. We don't even have the same doctor. I was leaving out and she was coming in. This was no coincidence. She had been looking for me for days. I knew it was God because he uses unexpected people to bless you. I had told God that I wanted to attend an event but had nothing to wear. This was on the morning of the event. He is such a faithful Father. The scripture says that He will supply all my needs. But do I always have to wait until the last second. It feels like I'm being stretched from the inside out. It is indeed very uncomfortable. Why can't God just say here daughter, go and get the things you need? Why can't everything I need just appear when I need it? That's what would happen if I were in control but I'm not. I am not confused about God being in control. I thank God for the trials because I keep getting stronger. I believe God is teaching me to trust only in him.

It's 3:00 in the morning and I'm not at peace in my spirit. I've wanted to move into my own place for several years now, but I was waiting on God. I'm growing weary of waiting. I'm experiencing some depression too. I don't want to jump ahead of God. I'm afraid of not doing something right. I've failed miserably in the past and I don't want that to happen again. I'm frustrated with my living arrangement and I can't take it much longer. I basically live in one room, so I won't get in the way. Every day I close the bedroom door behind me. This way I won't disturb anyone, nor will I be a target. But of course, even closing the door causes tension. I spend as much time as possible out of the house. I must shield myself from all the negativity around me. I've learned to guard my ear and eye gates. I'm living with the most negative person in my life and it's crushing. I often cry because I don't feel loved and it's my own family. I should have never been crying. It was the spirit of rejection. I should have taken authority over that spirit and cast it out in Jesus name. But all the while, I was waiting on God. He was waiting on me. This was something that he commanded me to do. Nevertheless, I want to leave so bad until it hurt inside. I will protect myself from negativity, hurt and disappointment. I'm trying not to go back to my old ways. I wish I could find the words to explain how difficult it is to live in this house. Everything I do is wrong or not good enough. I have no peace of mind and no joy here, but God is with me.

    I walk a lot, go to the YMCA and spend the night at my son's every chance I get. Anywhere must be better than where I am. The cost of living is high, much more than I can afford. I don't want to move into a low-income, drug infested place, but it's hard to be still. I can always go back to the apartments I lived in when I smoked crack. Deep down inside, I know that would be foolish. Sometimes I think I would be better off moving out and taking my chances. But I knew if I ever went back to the place God had delivered me out of, I would surely die. I had nowhere to go and it was safer where I was. I had to choose between crying every day or dying. I chose life so I stayed put.

Maybe God is trying to teach me how to wait. This is something I desperately need to master. It could change everything. Sometimes I simply must wait and that's all to it. Waiting is not an easy thing to do. Especially when things aren't going the way I think they should. When things get difficult, I always want to do something to make it better. My interference always makes it worse.

I began a fast two days ago but it was unsuccessful. I started again today, and I will be faithful to God. He is more important to me than anything. I want to hear him more clearly. I want to see and know the things that are going on around me. He calls for us to fast and pray so that's what I'll do. It seems like a thousand different things are happening at the same time. I'm not waiting on God, but He is so graciously waiting on me. He waits for me to be obedient to his will. He waits for me to live the way He commanded me to live. It is vital that I get in the word of God and keep my eyes on Him. Troubles are all around me. I am being pressed on every side, but I will not be crushed. It doesn't matter what it looks like because I walk by faith, not by sight.

I have discovered that keeping quiet and waiting on God is key. This will help me remain on the path God placed me. My words are much more power than I had realized. Long ago God told me that I talk too much. Since that time, I have been trying to remain quiet. I've made some progress, but I have a very long way to go. I talk all the time. I interrupt others when they are talking because I am so eager to talk. I prayed and asked the Lord to help me shut my mouth, yet I continue to talk too much. Too many words are a recipe for disaster. God told me I talk too much. It's because he's trying to help me stay on course to run my race.

The bible tells us that our words have power. ***Proverbs 18:21(NIV) "The tongue has the power of life and death, and those who love it will eat its fruit."*** God recently told me that He removed me from a job because I was talking too much. The confession that I was making out of my mouth was not His plan. My heart sank as I faced the reality that I had let God down again. I was talking so much that I was interfering with God's plan. But I am so grateful that He loves me. He didn't harm me nor destroy me. He simply moved me out of His way. I thank God for teaching me the way to go. There was so much confusion and chaos on that job. I must admit that I was a contributor to it. I should have kept my mouth shut and been in constant communication with God. I thought I was waiting for God to change the situation. But God was doing exactly what he wanted to do. His plan was working perfectly according to His will and not mine. I should have been praying and encouraging others. Instead I was acting like an unbeliever. I was waiting with the wrong spirit. I was walking around talking about God, but I was acting like the enemy. I'm not the boss, God is and I'm waiting to see His glorious plan fulfilled. I don't know what the plan is, but I know it's a good one. I could never figure out His plan. I'll keep walking in victory and help anyone I can along the way. I'm supposed to help God's people, not hinder them. I must consult God and pray to him constantly. He will lead and guide me around the obstacles and intrusions. Being in communication with God is key to living a successful life. God gave me a vision where I was standing on a mountain top. The sky was blue, and I could see a cloud or two in the distance. I inhaled the fresh, clean air and I had a smile on my face, and it was amazing. I felt light, carefree and peaceful. My arms were spread far apart like I was saying "I'm free." I wasn't afraid to look down, in fact I didn't even think about looking down. My eyes were gently closed, and I felt as light as feather. Oh, what an amazing God we serve.

Am I waiting on God or is he waiting on me? I won't stop spending time in God's presence. I won't stop digging into the scriptures. I'll keep listening to teachings on prosperity in the Kingdom. The blessing of the Lord maketh it rich and adds no sorrow to it. I realize that I must do the work. By that I mean, I must read my bible and meditate on the scriptures. I must open my mouth and speak the word of God in order to see it manifest in my life. If I say or do nothing, I'll have nothing. God made some promises and he watches over his word. His promises which are in His word shall remain the same. **Matthew 24:35(NLT) "Heaven and earth will disappear, but my words will never disappear."** I'm thankful that God is omnipresent. He knows my thoughts before I even realize what they are. Before I ask him for anything he's already there. He is always right on time. Thank you, God.

I've been so messed up in the past and it's by the grace of God that I'm here today. His patience and love for me are overwhelming at times. He has seen everything I've done, yet He holds me in his hands even now. He chose me; He called me in order to testify about his goodness. I am truly a new creature in Christ. He's not done with me yet. God could never let me down or disappointment me.

If only I could see how my bills will be paid every month, I would be so much happier. I keep thanking God for the things I have. I'm happier this year than I was last year. I must pray and ask God to give me more patience and he will. He'll do everything he said he would but, in his time, and not mine. I am very grateful to have a measure of patience. There was a time when I was one of the most impatient people ever. God says that I can ask him for anything I need. I must learn to be completely satisfied in any situation I'm in. I've lived paycheck to paycheck so long until somedays I ask when will it ever end? Recently I was so excited because I had placed all bills on my dresser. I prayed and asked God to pay them and I knew he would. Before I knew it, they had all been paid. I was so excited because I didn't have to wonder how it would be done. It was settled. The very next day I got a hospital bill in the mail. I had no idea how I would pay it. I thought, here we go again. The day after that I got a bill from my insurance company and I didn't know how I would pay that one either. Lord do I have to go through this for the rest of my life?

I sit here waiting for God's instructions. I don't know when or how he'll show up, but I know He will. God will never fail me. All my bills are due and some of them past due. It's hard to explain but I'm being squeezed. The more the bills fall behind the tighter the squeeze becomes. I will continue to tithe and walk in victory.

Money, money, money it always tries to distract me. Bills keep coming in and money continues to dwindle down. I wait on the Lord to show me which way to go. The Lord my God teaches me to profit and leads me along the way I should go. I thought God told me to give away some money, but I didn't do it. I was afraid to. But no good thing will He hold from them that walk uprightly. My sins are forgiven, and His grace is sufficient. I went to church with my neighbor tonight. I cried out to God and I heard him tell me, "you're more than a conqueror." He told me to know this scripture and I found it as soon as I got home. ***Roman 8:37 "Yet in all these things we are more than conquerors through Him who loved us."*** I'm not worried because God is my source. God told me that Jesus has already paid the debt.

WHAT CAME NEXT

Being a published author is a huge accomplishment. I couldn't have done it without the grace of God. I'm growing in my Christian walk and God is preparing me to fulfill my destiny. I know I'm getting closer to God. Walls that were erected to separate me from God are falling. Chains are being broken. Deliverance and healing are taking place in my life.

When God told me to write He also told me that He would open doors. I tried not to look at what others are doing. People told me what they did but God didn't tell me to do the same. I must use wisdom, so I ask God to give it to me. I know my books will accomplish what God sent them to do. That's all that matters. I always knew there would be more books to come. I knew it because I could feel something inside of me. It felt like another world existed in my belly. When God told me to keep writing it didn't come as a total surprise. But I didn't think it would happen so quickly. One day I sat down at the computer and began to push. I didn't know what would come out, but I knew I had to do it.

A few of my family members bought my book and I appreciate their support. However, most of them didn't even acknowledge that I had written a book. I admit at first it was a little disheartening, but ultimately it caused me to desire more of God. For that reason, I am thankful for the way it turned out. I told one cousin I had written a book and he said, "good for you!" I was no longer using drugs, but I wasn't treated much better by mother. It was because I had to prove that I wouldn't use again. In fact, my mother told me that she didn't trust me yet. I wanted to move away and not talk to them again. I knew this wouldn't help me heal nor was it God's will. I had to wait on God to do what only He could. If I moved away, I would be sabotaging my own Christian growth. I wanted to be delivered from this thorn in my side. So, I decided to wait for God to fix it all.

When I was in addiction, I had to wait on God to do what only He could. What if He had instantly delivered me when I asked him to? Would I have a real and effective testimony? I probably would have gone right back to using and perhaps even died. Trusting God and going through his process is the reason I'm alive today. I had to be willing to go wherever He sent me. Even though sometimes I was afraid I went anyway. My desire to be clean and to live life was greater than my fears. It was God who gave me the desire to want to live differently. Oh, what a mighty God I serve.

When God delivered me, I was consumed with guilt. I had messed up and I couldn't forgive myself. Everything the bible said not to do I had managed to do. I was overwhelmed with guilt because of how my children struggled. If only I didn't have sex until I was married, they would have had fathers in their lives. The enemy used condemnation against me. Condemnation heavy weight to carry and not from God. This was used against me because I didn't know the Word. There is no condemnation for them who are in Christ Jesus. It was horrible and for a while I was stuck right there. My children were fatherless. I couldn't imagine how they must have felt, and it was my fault.

Although I was physically there, I had checked out emotionally very early in their lives. I was determined to own up to what I had done. I was taking the blame for everything. It was my fault and I had to suffer because of it. My sons are both very fine young men, but I cannot take credit for that. God was their Father.

I was tormented by guilt. My children mean everything to me. I've prayed so often that God would turn their lives around. I've prayed and I wait to see something happen. Faith is not waiting to see something happen but knowing that it already has. I prayed according to the will of God so it shall come to pass. I can't sit around crying because that's unbelief. I trust God in all things. I was created for God's purpose and I won't be distracted. He has given me a set amount of time on earth to fulfil my destiny. I will never give up on God.

I know God loves my children because they belong to him. So, I must keep going. I'm waiting for things to change so I can live the good life. I was in my fifties before I got clean from drugs. I don't want to see my children live in darkness until they are fifty. I want them to live a blessed life. I want them to live an abundant life. I want God to heal and deliver them. I pray it all the time and then I wait.

God delivered me from drug addiction but not right away. The process of manifestation occurred over time. God loves my children just like he loves me. He is no respecter of persons. I look at my youngest son and I see that he lives in darkness just as I did. So smart and so talented, yet he remains in darkness. He could have so much, but he doesn't see it. He appears to be content right where he is, but I know that isn't the case. I know he has greatness inside of him and God has a good plan for his life. I'll keep praying and believing God will bring my son into the light. He's a good son and a good person. Right now, he is merely existing and not living. We wrestle not against flesh and blood but against principalities and spiritual wickedness in high places. This is a war that we're in and I will not take it lying down. I will fight with every breathe in my body.

My oldest son is my best friend. Many years passed and we didn't even speak to each other. I thank God for bringing us back together. He has so many struggles and I wish I could something to change it but only God can. I thought he had a food addiction, but God says it's unforgiveness. He's had way too many visits to the hospital for a young man. I believe God is healing and delivering him even now. He has been overweight for his entire adult life. My declaration is that he lives a long healthy, prosperous life, in Jesus name. Neither of my sons have been baptized yet but they will, in Jesus name. I realized how powerful they really are. My oldest son has a gift from God that even he doesn't fully understand yet. They will know the truth and the truth shall make them free. It doesn't matter what I did or didn't do with my children. I thank God that I'm not who I used to be. God is the light and in him there is no darkness. I know that no matter what it looks like, God is always with my children.

I see a lot of things happening with my grandson that I don't like. He has more people around for him than I ever did. This should be positive for him, but we made it negative. We had two different beliefs and we pounded him from both directions. I never want him to suffer in any way. I don't want any hinderances or stumbling blocks along the way for him. Of course, I want him to have a good life, better than the one I gave his dad. I am still guilty of slacking and not being all that I should be. I pray that God helps me to do better. I will continue to pray and trust God. I pray for my grandson and I pray with him. I used to wait until he went to bed, and I prayed alone. One day I heard a pastor say that we should pray with our children. It made sense because how would he learn to pray for himself. I held him in my arms, and we prayed together before bed. Now that he's older, I encourage him to pray for himself and others. I even talk to him about praying in tongues and I encourage him to do so.

   I was clean and I rededicated my life to the Lord, but nothing changed. I was angry, hurt, bitter and in so much pain. I was waiting for everyone to realize how they had hurt me. I was looking for sympathy and understanding. I wanted everyone to apologize for hurting me. But no one saw it my way and I was suffering inside. I realized I was trying to control others and I should have been asking God to change me. I was trying to please God and be committed to serving him. But I couldn't see how messed up I was inside. I was waiting on God to move in my life, but He was waiting on me. If I had done everything God told me to do; what would my life look like.

My pastor said that unforgiveness, bitterness and offense will block my blessings. I told myself that I had forgiven everyone who had hurt me. But the Holy Spirit convicted me every time the pastor mentioned it. I knew I hadn't forgiven because I could feel it inside of me. Every time she talked about unforgiveness; something would rattle inside me. I was saying it, but I didn't mean it. I wasn't ready to forgive. I was prepared to forgive under certain conditions only. I thought everyone needed to apologize to me and feel my pain. I was determined to stay angry until they could see what they did to me. I held on to anger until it began to weigh me down. I couldn't get any closer to God with this sin my heart, so it had to go. I started praying and asking God to help me to change. I told Him that I couldn't do it without Him. I confessed this sin and God is faithful and just. I didn't know how to talk to people that I was angry with. Anger and bitterness had attached itself to me and I couldn't shake it loose. Talking with someone who I was bitter and angry with was impossible. I found it to be just as difficult as not using drugs; I couldn't do it without God. When I repented from my heart, God began to deliver me from this brokenness. I stopped asking God to change others and I asked him to change me. This is when I began to see my circumstances changed.

   I had also been invaded by the spirit of rejection and that's a tough one. I was rejecting everything and everyone, including God. This sin had been in my heart for so long that it had taken root. I needed God to remove them. I went to my family members and tried to have conversations with them in hopes of restoring our relationship. But things went from bad to worse. Every attempt I made ended in disaster. We were worse off than before I started. I finally figured out that I had to wait on God. There was nothing I could do personally to resolves our issues. God could make all things new. God had to fix me first. One of the hardest things I've ever learned is to wait and do nothing.

I started to pray and ask God to change things. I thought if I prayed enough, I could rush God. But since God is not in time it didn't happen that way. God is not like us and I'm glad he isn't. It's not easy to wait because we were taught not to wait on anyone. I'm always waiting for God to tell me what to do next. He always has plenty for me to do. He knows what's next and when it's going to happen. I'll keep trusting him. An entire year is almost gone and yet it seems like one day.

I try to focus on His will for me. The bible says He will know me by my fruit, so I'll focus on that. I don't like to see anyone suffering or lost. I want to be on fire about my Father's business. The Father's business is winning souls for the Kingdom.

One day I stopped and talked with a woman who I had driven past for more than a year. She held up a sign saying she was homeless. A year ago, I'd given her a significant amount of money. I reminded her of it, and she was willing to talk with me. My first question was whether she knew Jesus and she said she did. She told me she had quit her job. I asked her why she wasn't living in a shelter. She said because they wouldn't allow her to stay with her husband. I spotted her husband hiding across the street. I talked and prayed with her and I wanted to do more. I decided to invite her to breakfast. It was winter and cold outside. She asked me where we would go? What a strange question for someone who was homeless and hungry. I named a restaurant, but she refused to go. How could a hungry person refuse a meal? It made no sense, so I went on my way. I'll never know the truth as to why she was there. So many people are on the street with signs saying they're homeless.

    There was a man who appeared to be homeless. I remember the first time I saw him. It was Thanksgiving Day and I was on my way to my aunt's house for dinner. I saw him standing on the side of a closed restaurant. I drove passed him, but I turned around. I went back to give him five of the ten dollars I had in my wallet. After that day I notice him all the time. He sat in front of a grocery store smoking cigarettes. I even prayed with him once. He was filthy and wore gloves with holes in them. He cursed a lot whenever we talked. He told me that he slept in the cemetery every night. I had great compassion for this man. One day I stopped and offered to get him a hotel room. I told him I would drop him off, pay for the room and pick him up at check-out. He refused to take the room. I didn't understand but I continued to try and help him. I asked him where I could meet him weekly to buy him food to eat. He told me he wasn't sure if he could meet me. After that I never offered to help him again. I've heard he died but I don't know for sure. I don't like to see people go without. I always try to help others and most of the time, I don't have much myself. I thank God that he has allowed me to see that not everything is like it seems. He told me to ask the people if they are saved and believe in Jesus Christ. Not only should I help them, but I should always tell them about Jesus. Many carry signs saying God bless you. But several times I've mention Jesus and they got angry and walked away.

My life is a fight and every day I prepare to step into the ring. I increase my prayer time and spend more time in the Word of God. I fight the good fight of faith. God has been propelling me into my purpose in the past three years. I've grown tremendously in such a short period of time. God is doing a new thing in my life. Not long ago, I was so afraid that I literally trembled when things happened to me. That was the spirit of fear and not from God. The devil had me terrified, but then I started to get the word inside of me. The enemy didn't want me to find out that the Greater One lives inside me. Jesus has already won the victory and I have nothing to fear. I'm never alone. Christ lives inside me and God will never leave nor forsake me.

I cried a lot and depended on other people to make the tears stop. But God has taught me a lot during these few years. At one time I was so afraid of God that I wouldn't say or do anything. I thought I would infuriate Him, and I never want to do that. He told me that I didn't know the Word and it was true. I told myself I would set aside time every day to spend in the Word. I haven't done it every day, but I'm trying. Some days I feel like I need more time praying. Other times I just want to be in the presence of God. I love the Lord so much and I want to be closer to him. He says to draw nigh to Him, and He'll draw nigh to me. The way to make that happen is spending time in the Word. God knows my heart. Even though I mess up, he knows how I love and adore Him. Because He knows, He teaches me how to get closer to Him. He said in His word, those who hunger and thirst for righteousness shall be filled. Thank you, God, for filling me up.

My pastor said that we should spend more time praying in the spirit. I thank God for the baptism of the holy spirit. I pray more in the spirit now and I believe it's helping. Why would I sit in church and listen but not apply the teaching to my life? My pastors are faith teachers. I can see how my faith has grown since they've been teaching me. Faith comes by hearing, hearing by the word of God. I have learned to watch the words that are coming out of my mouth. Life and death are in the power of the tongue. Throughout my life I have spoken many negative things over my life. Now that I know better, I do better. My pastors' have taught me to speak life over myself and over my children. They've taught me that I can speak life into any dead situation.

I looked for a job for a very long time and it was discouraging. I knew I was educated, qualified and experienced to do something. I finally found a job doing something I had never imagined. I was transporting consumers in a van. While I addicted, I'd spent countless hours riding on the city bus. I dated two bus drivers and regrettably rode around with them night and day. During this time, I learned a little about how to operate the controls on the bus. I could also fill out the paperwork. I didn't know at the time how significant this would be later in my life.

I started working and it was chaos from the beginning. I admit I was afraid to drive the van. I would be picking up and dropping off nine people every day. I had driven a car since I was sixteen but never anything this size. My coworkers were very bossy, and everyone was telling me what to do. The young lady who trained me told me no to worry about filling my paperwork out correctly. I disagreed with her. She complained to her boss, and I was called into the office. My supervisor told me that she received complaints that I refused to be trained. This made no sense and I explained that I would not falsify legal documents. She understood and sent me back out to do my job. They were upset because I wasn't fired, and I was upset because they plotted to have me fired. There was friction immediately on the job.

In the meantime, God gave me a dream that I would work for a company that had already refused to hire me. I didn't know how it would happen, but I believed what God had shown me. Two months after being employed as a driver, the vision God gave me began to manifest. The company was sold to the one God had shown me. I was in awe at what happened, and I thought I understood everything, but I was wrong. I was transferred to another location and things were even worse there. There was no structure, and no one knew what they were doing. My manager was late for work every day which meant my job was delayed too. No one seemed to care what time she arrived. All the employees walked on eggshells because of my supervisor. She was the author of a lot of confusion. She was not to be trusted. She could smile in your face and bite you in the back at the same time. In addition, there was blatant favoritism. But I continued to work there for two years.

One day I heard that the company was going to be sold again and I was confused. God had shown me this company so was I supposed to go with them or stay put? I didn't know what to do. I decided to apply for a position with the existing company. But they never contacted me, so I went with the new owners. Two months with the new owners and they announced that they would subcontract our driving positions.   I cannot and will not be anxious for anything because Jesus is Lord over my life. I was reminded that this is something I had been waiting for. I should be excited because I was going into a new season and meeting new people. I thought about how long I had been telling God that I felt it was time for me to move on and now it's happening. I must begin to use everything as an opportunity for growth. In this I'm reminded of ***Romans 8:28 (KJV) "and we know that all things work together for good to them that love God, to them who are the called according to his purpose."***

I had been telling my coworkers not to be surprised if they eliminated our positions. So, the news should not have been a surprise. Was it possible that in my spirit I knew what would happen?

    We went to a meeting with the owners of the transportation company. We filled out applications and went for interviews. But they never offered me a job and I was under pressure. I had accepted an apartment, so I needed a job. I recalled an acquaintance of mine had a friend who needed a driver for her daycare. We set up an interview and I was hired immediately as a driver. I began working at the daycare immediately and I was relieved to have a job.

    Things did not happen the way they were supposed to. I found out that the daycare had a bus and not a van. This meant that I would have to upgrade my license from Chauffer's License to a Commercial Driver's License. I prepared to do it, and I thought it would be simple. In the meantime, I volunteered to pick the children up from school in my personal vehicle. This wasn't good because my car was leased and over the allowed mileage. This was a nightmare, but I was confident it would only be a couple of weeks. I would get my CDL license and legally drive the daycare bus. But I failed the test miserably. I didn't want to take it again because it was much more difficult than I had anticipated.

I asked my boss if I could work inside the daycare and she said yes. I wasn't prepared for what would happen next. There was constant confusion. They daycare operated out of three trailers. Each staff member was assigned to a trailer. Each trailer held a different age group of children. One day I reported to work in trailer one. The next day the state shut it down, and everyone was moved. Everything was constantly shifting. We were changing buildings and changing children. I didn't like it one bit. I was becoming bitter and rebellious. I was uncomfortable with the constant changes. Then one day God sent me a message. He said he's is the boss. When the course of my day changes, I should consult him. Because He is doing something good in my life. I knew I had to calm down and stop being upset. Afterall it's about him and not me.

I worked at the daycare for about a month when I started receiving phone calls from my old coworkers. They told me that the company decided not to subcontract our jobs and I could come back to work. I held my head and I wanted to scream. So much confusion around me, yet I felt I was in the right place. I didn't understand and I didn't like it. But I knew to stand still. Later, God told me that He had to move me because I was talking too much. I was saying the wrong things. I don't know what's next for me, but I know it's good, because it will be from God.

I began to ask God to change me. I asked him to change my attitude and help walk in love. I prayed for him to show me how to adapt to the changes. I had to be a good servant, I wanted to please God. I did not want to be difficult or operate in the wrong spirit. Things did get better because God helped me. I'm still at the same job and it's been almost seven months. Believe it or not but things are still constantly changing. But I thank God that I'm no longer rebellious and bitter about the changes. I realize that life changes and I can't be shaken or distracted by it.

The enemy is constantly trying to put sickness in my body. I am healed by the stripes of Jesus. I woke up one morning with lower back pain. It had to be the enemy because I hadn't injured myself. Somehow, somewhere a door had been opened and sin entered in. I confessed the word of God that I am healed by His stripes. But the pain didn't leave right away. I have power over the enemy, so I continued confessing the word of God. The next morning, my back hurt for several hours before the pain subsided. I kept confessing and believing the word of God that I'm healed. I went to bed and was only able to sleep about two hours before I was awakened in pain. I prayed in the spirit and spoke the word of God, but the pain persisted. I tried to sit up in a chair, but it wasn't comfortable. I was awake all night. I went to church and the pastor was teaching on healing. I didn't hear a word he said. The pastor had altar call, but I was serving others and unable to go. First service was over, and I was ready to serve again. Fortunately, one of the ladies offered to take my place. I had planned to visit an open house after church with my sister, so I went home. Something was telling me to stay and listen to the teaching. But I didn't stay because I had already made up my mind. I was being disobedient. God was trying to help me, but I did what I wanted to do. I should have been ecstatic to sit and listen, but I left anyway. I had been praying but when God answered me, I walked away. I cannot ask for God's help and then ignore him when He answers.

I went to work on Monday and the pain seemed to subside. Around bedtime fear began to overtake me. I remembered the night before and I didn't want to experience the same pain. The enemy tried to convince me that I needed a new mattress. The Holy Spirit reminded me that Jesus slept soundly in a boat. Jesus slept during a storm so I could certainly sleep in my bed. I began to boldly confess healing over my body in Jesus name. Nevertheless, at bedtime I prepared to sleep sitting up in the living room. I nodded off on two separate occasions but didn't sleep very long. I was so tired from being awake the night before. Something happened inside me, so I got up and went into my bedroom. I anointed my head with blessed oil. I prayed, then I got into my bed and went to sleep. God, I thank you that I'm healed.

My pastors taught me that God gave man dominion. When I feel something in my body that doesn't belong, I take authority over it. One day I went to the bathroom and I saw something strange. I was concerned but I didn't say anything. It got worse and I told my mother about it.   She thought it was horrible. She told me what she thought it looked like and it didn't sound good. I made an appointment with the doctor and he ordered a test. When I went in for the results, he said I was fine.   By then the symptoms had gone away.   Two weeks later the symptoms reappeared but this time I didn't tell anyone. Every time I saw the symptoms, I said I am healed. Then one day I went to the altar at church. I asked for prayer for my finances. I should have been going for healing because of this condition. But I wasn't thinking about the condition. We prayed and the pastor walked by and laid his hands on me.   I felt a warm sensation go through my body. Instantly, I was reminded of the condition. Somehow, I knew I was healed. I never saw the symptoms again.

I've wanted to move out on my own for a very long time. Prior to my deliverance from addiction,

I moved to Minnesota and lived in someone's home. I lived there for 18 months. When it was time to move back to Indiana, I moved in with my mother which I was very reluctant to do. I still had a lot of issues going on within me. I wanted to be happy and I didn't think it would happen there. I went anyway knowing it's what God wanted me to do.

I waited for God to show me where to go and He finally did. My spiritual mom showed me some apartments under construction. We spoke to a man who said the waiting list was two years long. I decided to put my name on the list anyway. In three months, they called and said I could apply for an apartment.

I quickly went in and filled out an application. They told me they would process it and call. I was so excited until they called and said they were rejecting my application. I cried for the rest of that day. I had given up on moving because I was exhausted. I told my girlfriend what happened, and she encouraged me to keep fighting. I'm glad I listened to her because they approved my application. They would do an employment verification right away to complete the process. But then I received another negative call. Now there was a discrepancy in my employment information. I called my employer and asked them to send the correct information. Finally, the application process was completed. The devil tried to keep me out of that apartment, but God is bigger. The enemy will never stop throwing fiery darts in your path. I put on the whole armor of God.

New Year's Day I spent my first night in the apartment. I was so excited not to be shut up in one room. It was wonderful not to answer to someone else for everything I did. This was my apartment and I could do as I pleased. It was peaceful and I was content. Although I live alone, it's a different alone than before. I have freedom here. I'm able to do the things that I want to do how I want to do them. I still desire a husband and I believe he too will come. I was grateful even though the apartment was completely empty.

It was brand new and no one had ever lived in it before. I know with God all things are possible. I didn't have any furniture and no visible means of getting any. But through a program at church, someone gave me a dining room set. At first, I refused it because it was so large. But I realized having something beats nothing at all. Then I applied for a charge card at a furniture store and I got a bedroom set. I didn't know how I would pay for it, but I knew God would make a way. Next, someone gave me bunkbeds for my grandson's room and my son bought the mattresses. I was praying everyday thanking God for my living room furniture. Today I got a call saying someone wanted to donate a couch and love seat to me. Isn't God wonderful. All I had to do was pick up the furniture and it would be mine free of charge. I don't own a truck and I cannot load or unload furniture. But I believed God would make a way. God showed me who to call so my couch and loveseat were delivered.

    I knew I had to keep my faith working for the things I needed. I woke up at night and didn't know the time. I needed a clock in my bedroom. I wondered whether I should buy one to sit on the chest or a wall clock. I planned on going to the second-hand store to look around. But God had a better plan for me. A friend of mine was moving and she invited me over. She said God told her to give me a plant. I looked at some of the items she had for sale, but nothing stood out. I was walking out of the room and I saw a clock. I bought it for only five dollars. I plugged it in and tried to set the time but I couldn't. I began to get a little irritated, so I left it alone. I called my friend and asked her if she would help me with the clock. She gave me the operating instructions. My neighbor helped me figure it out. She told me that this clock was a treasure. She said the clock was worth much more than I paid for it. Then she said, "all you said was that you wanted a clock." I began to cry because God is so faithful. A week prior one of my sister's in Christ whispered in my ear, "you have a blessing coming." This was a blessing from God. It was so much more than just a clock. I was able to play music and sermons through the clock speakers. The favor of God was working in my life. I had an apartment full of furniture, most of which was given to me. God is great and greatly to be praised.

Just when things are going so well the attacks begin. Always the same things, he never has any knew strategies. But he is nothing more than a big liar. He's already defeated by Jesus Christ, my Lord, my Redeemer. The enemy talks all the time unless I shut Him up with the word of God. He puts thoughts in my mind the minute I open my eyes in the morning. God's word says in **2 Corinthians 10:5 (NIV) *We demolish arguments and every pretension that sets itself up against the knowledge of God, and we take captive every thought to make it obedient to Christ.***

When I didn't know what to do, I would do nothing. I was just where the devil wanted me to be. But I thank God I know more now than I used to. He knows how much I love the Lord. The enemy worked overtime to keep me in fear. I used to be afraid of the devil. I cried a lot and never open my mouth to fight back. I didn't resist because I didn't know how. God said my people perish for lack of knowledge and I was in trouble. This whole time he was afraid of me and I didn't know it. The enemy was terrified that I would find out the truth. I have authority over all the power of the enemy. He cannot harm me. His weapons will not prosper against me. When I talk about the blood of Jesus or the name of Jesus the devil flees. God told me, "when he strikes, you strike back." When the enemy opens his mouth, I open mine and release the Word of God. My pastors taught me that I don't fight the devil. I fight the good fight of faith. Faith comes by hearing and hearing by the Word of God. I listen to the word and I speak when trouble comes. Sometimes I forget to use the word when trouble comes, fear overpowers my words. This means my roots are not deep enough. I must read it again and hear it again until it's hidden in my heart.

    Now I'm clear that I must wait on the Lord. It's not something that comes easily all the time. I thank God for his grace and mercy. I thank him because he is so patient and loving. I thank him because he is the great "I AM." He is everything I need. I thank him because the blood of Jesus covers me. The healing power is in His blood. I thank him because he meets me right where I am. He doesn't hold my past against me. I thank him for meeting me in my secret place. I can tell him all the things I feel inside, and He won't abandon me. Even when I don't understand why I feel the way I do. I can confess to him that I don't want to feel this way anymore. I repent and ask him to heal the wounds in my heart. My God knows just what I need. He will never deny me anything that lines up with his word. He gives me assignments and leads me along the way I should go. If I am obedient, I will continue to grow and walk with the Lord. Sometimes I get in God's way because I don't wait for Him. He'll never fail me, and he won't let me fall. I ask God to give me more patience. This way I will always wait on Him. I can see and feel growth taking place in my life. I know God is watching over me. He's teaching and molding me into the woman of God he created. Because I was not always in his will, somethings got out of alignment. But the blood of Jesus redeemed me. I understand why God was telling me that I don't know the Word. The word is God, so I didn't know him. He speaks to me and gives me revelation through his word.

   I must go through every season with joy, love and peace in my heart. I will not complain as I go from season to season.   Some seasons will not be as pleasant as others. I spend more time in the wilderness than I'd like to. I'm sure it's somewhat because of my laziness. My life is not my own. God created me for his purpose and plan. I am in this world but not of this world. This morning I was reading my bible in the book of Matthew in chapter 26. It said that Jesus became anguished and distress about what was going to happen to him. ***Matthew 26:39(NLT) declares, He went on a litter farther and bowed with his face to the ground, praying, "My Father! If it is possible, let this cup of suffering be taken away from me. Yet I want your will to be done, not mine."*** Jesus knew he would be betrayed and killed, and he became anguished about it. He was always about his Father's business. He released those feelings and immediately said "your will be done." I think about all the complaining I do when things get tough. The more I complain, the more difficult it becomes to walk it out.

My hearts' desire is to be closer to God. I will pray, fast and study the word more often. This must be the one sure way to hear God more clearly. I have so many questions for God. I must be sure that I can hear him when he answers me. I bind the spirits of distraction and confusion, in Jesus name.

Sometimes I can't wait. I must always be active because time stands still for no one. Faith is an action word and the scriptures say to walk by faith. It does not say stand still and wait by faith. Things are happening all around me and I must keep walking. If I stop, I may not reach my destiny, so I'll keep going. Darts are being thrown at me constantly. Some days I ask God to give me the strength to get up. Health, finances and confusion are areas where the enemy tries to come in. But thank God that the Greater One lives inside me. Clearly, I'm not doing something right. I should not continue to be attacked in the same areas. This morning before I got out of bed, I listened to faith teachings. I had to build my spirit man up for the day. I listened as I made my bed and showered. Then I was eager to spend time praying and listening to God. He is the only one who can give me instructions and directions. He told me what to do. Immediately the enemy was telling me to do something else. But I knew which direction I had to go.

This is a time of learning and growing in my life. I had so many ways that were ugly and not of God. God has so much work to do in me and I'm grateful he loves me unconditionally. Sometimes others can see what is happening in my life before I do. I'm grateful they help me along the way. I can see growth and change taking place in my life and spirit. I am becoming spiritually mature, but I have a long way to go. I thank God that I'm no longer a baby in Christ.

People tell me that I'm pushy when I talk to others about God. I didn't think I was, but they must be right. Several people have told me the same thing. I thought I changed but I continue to hear the same thing. I don't know why I do it, but I don't want to. I don't want to push anyone away from God. I can't force something on them that they're not ready to receive. Things happen in God's time and in God's way not mine. God help me to keep my mouth shut. Guard my mouth and keep watch over the doors of my lips Lord.

The process of being changed by God is long and exciting. I'm so glad that He is faithful to do everything he says he will. God knows how I desire to please him. I know everything that's not like God must go. I'm glad I gave my life to the Lord. I have a hunger and thirst for him. I didn't even realize that evil was residing inside me. Now that God has changed me, I can feel when something is not right. I pray and ask God to fix me and He always does. He so graciously points out the things that have me puzzled. Sometimes I don't like my ways. Everything that will separate me from God must go. I need more of him. I love him so much. When I see that He is speaking to someone else, I want to hear him just as they do. He is my Father and I want to talk with him every day. How will I know what to do if I don't ask him or if I'm unable to hear him?

My attitude was horrible, but it wasn't too difficult for God. He is bigger than any circumstance. Spending time in the word, fasting and praying are very important for my walk with God. Do I utilize them as I should? No, I don't but I always try to do better. I know God was teaching me how to fast and I was progressing. I went from a one day fast, to a three day fast, to a seven day fast. I fasted for seven days and I could hear God speaking clearly. I didn't even have to ask a question for Him to speak to me. It was amazing, just what I had been seeking. That was two months ago, and I haven't done it since.

Sometimes it seems like I just can't get started. It's not because I don't want the relationship with God because I do. I love God so much that when I don't hear from him it makes me want to cry. I'll always seek to be closer to God.

WAITING FOR GOD

For so many years my life consisted of getting up, going out and doing what I needed to do. Basically, I've been alone since I was 19 years old. I didn't do much waiting because I couldn't. If I didn't do it, it would not get done. I refused to wait because I had been let down so many times. If I asked someone to help me and was told to wait, I did it myself. In my mind wait, meant no!

Waiting was painful because of the fear of rejection. I explored other options rather waiting. If I failed on my own, it didn't hurt as bad as being lied to or let down. I never understood why people couldn't say what they meant. I don't know why my mind was so messed up. It could have been from being let down so many times. The spirit of rejection is nasty. Unless you've experienced it, you could never understand. I had two children with two fathers who never helped take care of them. It doesn't get more painful than that. I often needed help that never came. So many were depending on me, but I had no one to depend on.

I must wait for everything I want. People around me are getting the desires of their hearts so why can't I? God told me not to settle and I realize I must keep my faith working. God promises me in ***Psalms 84:11 (NLT) For the LORD is our sun and shield; He gives us grace and glory. The LORD will withhold no good thing from those who do what is right.*** I must stop praying for what I want and pray for God's will to be done. Material things are so unimportant because people are perishing right in front of me. Focusing on things of this world, distracts me from doing God's will. He's a good Father and He already knows what I need.

I ask God to help me wait and not complain. I ask God what to do and He answers. Then I start to complain about the route He shows me. I ask God to help me wait with joy in my heart and not anger. When I'm going through a trial, complaining leaves an opening for the enemy.

I cannot express how important it is to always wait on God. In all things we must seek Him first. It's impossible to do without faith and knowledge of the word of God. We must know what the promises of God are and believe they are true. Throughout the ministry of Jesus many people suffered, but their faith healed them. I was on drugs and living recklessly. I thought I wouldn't be set free, but God was teaching me faith. As I began to cry out to Him for help, he used people to tell me to trust Him.

God loved me even when I was in my mess. I must have faith in God. I must wait until He fixes me. I pray according to His will, He hears me, and I have the petitions of my prayer. I pray for a long prosperous life for my family and me. We are mighty men and women of God. We have godly children that love the Lord. I speak long life and blessings over us, in Jesus name.

Some days I get weary because things don't seem to change. At times I don't want to talk to anybody but God. He's the boss and knows everything. He reminds me of the things he's already done for me. He reminds that He's delivered me out of darkness. I lived a life of destruction for many years. I don't wish that on anyone, especially not my children. It's difficult for me to see anyone suffering. I can't focus on what I see instead I believe what God says. I think about who God created me to be.

   I must forgive others immediately because God forgave me. When I pray the spirit of truth will tell me what he's heard. He will tell me things to come. I must wait on God because he can change anything. God tells me what to do while I wait for him to deliver and set the captive free. Holding on to unforgiveness gives sickness permission to enter my body. I refuse to allow the enemy to put sickness in my body. I ask God to show me anyone who I haven't forgiven. I must forgive them for God to forgive me. I release unforgiveness, anger, bitterness and offense now. God, I ask you to wash and cleanse me of all unrighteousness.

   Sometimes frustration and heaviness try to overtake me. Nothing ever seems to go right, but

I still wait on the Lord. I'm lost without him and I don't know what to do next. Many times, I get in His way. Of course, it's unintentional but I must move over.

God has shown me so many things that I have not seen come to pass yet. Once He showed me a building and simultaneously, He put an idea in my mind. I walked back and forth in front of the building and prayed. I thanked God for giving me the business. I took pictures and I could see the business manifesting in the spirit. I printed out the pictures and put them on a poster board. I needed to remind myself of my new business. I wanted it to get deep down in my spirit. That was several months ago. Now it looks like someone bought the building. The "for sale" sign has been taken down and lights are on inside the building. In the past I would have forgotten all about it, but I know better. I must wait on God's timing because it's perfect. I don't know how or when, but I know that He will. I didn't ask God for this but I'm very clear on what He said. I won't walk around anxious or worrying about when it will happen. I'll keep seeking God and His will every day. I'll continue to walk along the path in which He guides me. There is no turning back now. He leads and I follow. He is the Lord my God who teaches me to profit and leads me along the way I should go.

Sometimes God tells me to do things and I hesitate. Not because I want to but for different reasons. Sometimes it's fear and sometimes it's confusion. I'm not certain it's God. I don't want to make a mistake; I want to get it right. It's very important that I go when God tells me to. Sometimes it seems like God has left me when I don't hear from Him. I can't just pick up and start doing things on my own. I'll wait until He gives me instructions on what to do next. I'll keep doing what He told me last. I'll use the wisdom and remain in His will. He says stand still and know that I am God. He tells me in His word to be anxious for nothing and pray about everything. I'll wait on God.

Waiting on God is the key to living the life He created for me. I appreciate everything God does. Every good gift and perfect gift come from above. Thank you for waking me up another day in my right mind. Thank you for introducing me to people with the same experiences that I have had. Thank you for connecting me to women of God who will help lead me into my next season. Teach me Father, to always look through my spiritual eyes and not the natural. Thank you for carrying me through the rough times. Thank you for tearing down strongholds. I am the righteousness of God in Christ Jesus. Yeah though I walk through the valley of the shadow of death I will fear no evil, for though art with me. Thy rod and thy staff they comfort me. The enemy seeks to devour me, but I come boldly to the throne of grace that I may obtain mercy and find grace to help in time of need. I shall wait upon the Lord and He will renew my strength, I will mount up on wings like eagles; I will run and not get weary, I will walk and not faint. When I wait on the Lord, I am certain to be on the right path. Waiting is not always easy because of the thoughts the enemy puts in my mind. Sometimes he tells me that I'm waiting too long. It's a lie every time. The enemy will never tell the truth.

   I could make a list of things that I've been praying for and have not received. The list would be enormous. I just want to cry sometimes. But then I remember how truly blessed I am. He woke me up this morning. He woke up every member of my family today. People are dying all around me but I'm still alive. I'm in my right mind and I have full use of all my limbs. I am so grateful to be blessed. I have a roof over my head and a bed to sleep in. I have a job and a car, thank you Lord for all you've done for me.

I cannot weaken, and I must remain strong. I ask the Lord to strengthen me daily. The joy of the Lord is my strength. God has everything I need. I ask Him to sustain me so I can keep moving forward. The devil can't harm me because the Greater One lives inside me. Jesus has already won the victory over the enemy. Sometimes I feel like He's always messing with me and I never get a break. I know God is fighting my battles and I'm fighting too. I'm fight the good fight of faith.

If only God would help me understand what is happening right now. If only He would tell me how to break these chains. Something is wrong because I'm not getting any manifestation. I continue to tithe, and I have given a lot. I've sown into the lives of others and have reaped no harvest. God says, "as long as the earth remains, they'll be seed time and harvest." Lord help me because I'm walking by sight and not faith as you commanded. The woman in the bible with the issue of blood was bleeding for twelve years. I know everything doesn't happen instantly, but God please help me. I pray every day and I ask God to lead me and to guide me, but I get impatient. When He doesn't answer right away, I forget what I've asked Him to do. One day He told me that I don't even remember what I've prayed for. Once I did something and I heard God say, I didn't tell you to do that. I had to repent for being self-righteous. I'm so grateful that God corrects me and teaches me.

The more determined I am to wait for God to speak to me, it seems like the worse I do. Recently I've been losing money by doing things that I believe are faith moves but each time I get negative results.

There was an event and I really felt that I should attend. The host was a radio personality and author. She was hosting an author's brunch in a major city. I thought this was my chance to meet people just like myself. I prayed about it, but I never heard from God. I knew financially I couldn't do it. But God is rich, and he can do anything. I paid the deposit and waited for God to provide everything I needed for the trip. I convinced myself that I heard God tell me to go. Surely, He would supply all I needed because it was an assignment from him. I continued to trust in him.

As the deadline grew near, I was no closer to having the money for the trip. I still didn't give up because I know God is able. The entire time I was very careful to watch the words coming out of mouth. I confessed that I was going to the brunch. I really thought I would be there. I was determined not to worry about when it would happen. My only job was to keep believing that it would. Finally, I began to pray that God's will be done and not mine. I asked God to show me which way to go. His yoke is easy, and His burden is light. I don't have to toil for anything. I was anxious and afraid. I was feeling everything but faith. I continued to say I trusted God but deep down inside I really didn't. Looking back, I can say that I was more afraid than anything. I was afraid that God wouldn't do it and faith is knowing He will.

The deadline was getting closer to pay the balance. I fought even harder to believe God would. I received a message from the host reminding me to pay the balance. I didn't know what to tell her. I know that my words have power. I couldn't say I was going, and I couldn't say I wasn't. It was very exhausting. I was determined to fight the "good fight of faith." Now it was the day before the money was due. I could no longer ignore the host, so I asked God what to say. I didn't hear him answer. I told her that I could not attend due to circumstances beyond my control. Now I was ashamed and embarrassed. It would have been easier to wait until I heard from God. Moving ahead of God makes things so difficult. While going through this the enemy tried to put sickness in my body. I had to resist that as well. Through it all I still trusted Him. I didn't get to go to the event, and I lost my deposit. I had done something out of the will of God. I thank him for protecting me from myself. Lord help not to yield to my flesh.

I won't do things on my own because it's so chaotic. I recall the saying "wait broke the wagon." I used to repeat this saying but not anymore. Those that wait upon the Lord, shall renew their strength is what the Word says. As a child my parents told me to learn to do things for myself. This way I wouldn't have to depend on anyone. I continue to get closer to God and learn his will. Now I can see that the enemy planted lies in my mind. God clearly tells us to trust and depend on him. Due to lack of knowledge people continued to repeat these sayings. Some never realize that words have power. Sometimes as I try to wait on God, I can feel my flesh rising. The feeling of wanting to do something becomes overwhelming. If I'm waiting on God and I get anxious or nervous I need to pray. God tells me to be anxious for nothing. If I'm worrying, I'm not in faith. I'll keep listening to the word of God because the scriptures say in **Romans 10:17 (KJV) *So then faith cometh by hearing, and hearing by the word of God.***

As I wait upon the Lord, others pass me by. The things I'm wait for they already received. I'm happy for them, but at the same time I want it too. What I'm saying is that I want a good life too. They say it's not my time yet but when will my time come? I try not to complain because God is so good to me. I don't understand his reasons, but I know it's all for the best. I'm reminded of a story in the bible of the man who was crippled for 38 years so how can I complain. Who am I to complain about what God is doing? I'll wait because what God has is better than anything I could imagine. He's worth the wait. The world says, "if you want something done right, do it yourself." God says to trust in him and follow his ways and not ours. I must come to the place of total surrender.

I never stopped going to church, although I was not reading the bible very often. I heard that faith without works is dead. I kept messing up because I didn't have the revelation. I kept getting in God's way stepping further away from a breakthrough.

One of the areas I didn't receive a breath through was in my finances. I always wanted to be a giver and a tither. It has been a very discouraging journey for me. I learned the hard way to seek God. I have nothing negative to say about pastors or their teaching about giving. Each person is responsible to read the word for themselves. The bible says in **2 Corinthians 9:7 (NLT) *You must each decide in your heart how much to give. And don't give reluctantly or in response to pressure. "For God loves a person who gives cheerfully.*** I wait on God to lead me in this area as well. I was at church when collected offering after offering. The pastor said the money would return to me multiplied. I was eager to give it. I was already a tither. I wanted to do everything I could to honor God. I gave until I had nothing left but I didn't get it back. God didn't multiple it like the pastor said and I was confused. This rendered me afraid and confused. I've listened to preaching and teaching that instructed me to give. I wanted to please God, so I did what they said. However, I wasn't studying it out for myself. I never stopped giving but I gave reluctantly. This was against the word of God. I would never reap a harvest this way. I wasn't a cheerful giver; in fact, I was terrified. I was afraid that I wouldn't have enough to pay my bills or eat. It's all about trusting in God and not man. I had to know the word. Giving comes from the heart and not from someone pulling on your pocket. I was digging a hole for myself and didn't even know it.

When I tapped into God's will concerning giving, I stopped giving in fear. I began to give more. I even gave to different ministries. I needed to operate in the principle of sowing and reaping.

One day I needed some help paying a bill. It was not a large amount, but I didn't have it. I went to my church to ask for help. They rejected my application. My first reaction was to get angry, but I knew I couldn't. I didn't want to be bitter or offended. So, I went back to the assistant pastor. He said he knew I was a tither and a giver, but the church couldn't help me. He told me in so many words that maybe I was giving too much. He said to make sure I paid my bills before giving to others. I almost got offended because I do pay my bills. What was he thinking saying this? The church gives away $25 gift cards to people for visiting the church. I couldn't receive help and I was a tithing member. I didn't understand how they could turn me down. This was the opposite of what the head pastors were teaching. They said if I didn't have enough to meet my needs "sow a seed." God would increase it and supply my needs. After this I pulled back on my giving, but I continued to tithe. I could no longer do what they were asking but I had to seek God on giving. In seeking God, I learned to wait on him. He will tell me when, where and how much to sow. I learned that God anoints leaders and teachers, but He is still the boss. I will always consult him for instructions.

Should I be waiting on God even for giving? I was taught growing up not to wait on anyone. I was expected to learn to do things for myself. This was drilled in me so how could I now wait on God. It could only come by the renewing of my mind. God will graciously do it if I ask him. It's a process I'm going through. I love the changes God is making in me. Not because I think I'm so much better than I used to be; even though I am. But the most important thing is knowing God is pleased with me. I submit myself to him and allow him to renew my mind. Then he'll be able to use me for his purpose. Waiting on God is everything because his timing is perfect. Sometimes I pray and ask God for things and it seems like nothing changes. It seems like he's not answering my prayers. But as soon as I pray, God answers. I went to the altar for prayer and a lady said, "God told me to tell you that every delay works in your favor." I heard it, I received it and I believe it. Hearing from God causes me to rest and not be anxious for anything. Sometimes I just want God to say something to me. It doesn't even matter what it is. I only want to hear his voice.

I talk to God about my desire to hear from him more and have conversations with him. I shouldn't be anxious; I should be praying because anxiety hinders conversations with God. It's not easy to wait when you don't know what you're waiting for. It seems like I've been waiting my whole life. I've been waiting to live, and I still feel like I'm a long way from it. I think I've always known that my life was supposed to be very good. But there were many problems along the way.

I don't know how much longer I have on the earth. I'm getting older and so is everything around me. I look out the window and everything is ugly, dead and abandoned. The trees are dead, and the branches are falling. The buildings and houses are not being cared for anymore. People just walk away and leave them. No one is held accountable for their actions anymore.   It's sad as I look all around and wonder when my life will begin. How much longer do I have to wait for changes to take place? I continue to go to church and I believe God is everything that he says he is. He is in total control of everything because he created all things. I'm not the same person I used to be, although I'm still pretty messed up. There are so many cliques and so much favoritism. I don't feel like I really belong anywhere. I think I'm okay not being in a clique but how do I live my life. This Christian walk can be overwhelming sometimes. It seems like something should be happening, yet it's not.

    I heard God say, ***Psalms 37:4(KJV) "Delight thyself also in the LORD; and he shall give thee the desires of thine heart."*** My next thought was, the devil knows scripture too. I still didn't know what to do or how to feel. I laid there in silence for a few moments. I turned the television on and the first scripture I saw ***was Psalms 37:4***

Delight thyself also in the LORD; and he shall give thee the desires of thine heart. This was confirmation that if I trust God, he will bless me. God told me "I can't bless you until you get out of the way." I must keep moving forward. The same opportunities will come again. But I wish I had gotten it right the first time. Lord help me to get it right. God says that He shall supply all my needs, so I must stay out of his way. There's no way I should be scuffling and counting every penny I get. My God is a God of abundance, plenty and overflow. I am the head and not the tail. I am above only and not beneath. I'm blessed going in and coming out. I can say scriptures, but they must get into my heart.

For about three years I've belonged to a prayer group. One of the ladies whispered to me one day "invite me to the wedding?" Well when is that going to be? I believe God said something to her about it, but I'm still waiting. Some days I ask God if he would just give me one thing? It seems as if I'm waiting for so much and getting nothing. I'm still waiting on a relationship with my mother. It hasn't happened yet, and I don't know if it ever will. I no longer cry about it but sometimes it still hurts. I'm grateful that God has been so good to me. I know better than anyone how blessed I am. But until I receive the promises of God, I won't stop seeking him.

My whole life I've been waiting to live and now that I am, I want more. This is only the beginning of what God has in store for me. God has shown me many things that have yet to happen. Some of what I've seen, I don't understand at all. All I can do is wait. God has already preordained it to come to pass. He has given me names of people and places. I have yet to meet these people or visit the places.

One night I was sleeping, and God gave me some numbers. I thought it was a phone number. I dialed the number, but it was not in service. I know God will reveal what the number is. Lord I wish I had the answers now. What is the point of having information I can't use? Nevertheless, I will wait.

I wait for the purpose of my life to be revealed. The anticipation of not knowing what's next causes anxiety. I'm thankful each day God wakes me up because he doesn't have to. I'm grateful that he wakes up every member of my family because he chooses to. I'm happy that I'm still able to open my eyes and see all God's creations. I must keep walking otherwise I'll never arrive. I will reach my destiny. I'm not afraid of what is to come. God has not given me a spirit of fear. My life could be over at any time. I could lose everything like **Job** did. I must have unshakeable faith. I must always be alert and watching. I'm forever grateful.

It seems that I've spent more time in life waiting than anything else. I overcome an obstacle then I wait for God's next instruction. I should celebrate each victory no matter how small it may seem. The adversary is lurking, seeking to devour me. Everyday I'm waiting for God. I walk on eggshells because I don't want to do the wrong thing. I don't want to disappoint God. I'm always excited to see what God has in store for me next. My life keeps getting better and better. Sometimes I look at my life in the natural. That's when it looks like a "natural disaster." My spiritual eyes can see the truth. Walking in the spirit allows me to see all that God is showing me. I am a spirit being. God speaks to my spirit, not my flesh. I don't want to miss the next instruction from God. I wait with a spirit of expectancy. I will receive all that God has promised me.

Without faith it is impossible to please God. Faith is hoping for something even though you don't see it. I will trust God and His word while I wait for it to manifest in my life. I walk by faith because I know the word of God is true.

I have been deceived all my life to operate in time. God is not in time. We want God to do things instantly for us. When we pray, believe and do not doubt. Receive it when you pray because it's already done. When we don't see it immediately, we assume God didn't hear us. The enemy will try to convince us that God is angry with us. Therefore, he won't answer our prayers. This is a lie from the pit of hell. It's important that we study the Word. Then the enemy cannot convince us that his lies are the truth. Trusting God still means waiting on God. He moves in his own time and his own way. He didn't delivery me from drugs overnight, but He did deliver me. I couldn't see that He was working things out. But he was, from the moment I asked him to. I was hysterical and desperate while I waited. I made it worse on myself. I couldn't see how I would ever stop using drugs; I only knew I wanted to stop. I was hopeless and had no faith. I didn't even know what faith was. I didn't wait with the expectation that God would deliver me. But he is merciful and delivered me anyway.

I was talking with my co-worker and she said, "you're not on this job for the reason you were hired." She was talking and I was listening because I knew it was prophetic. She said I was there to tell somebody something. She told me that I would figure it out. Things on the job are not lining up. I thought about trying to figure it out on my own but that would be trouble. I must wait on God and He'll tell me who, what, when and where.

I'm waiting on my life to happen. I'm waiting for change and victories in every area of my life. I'm waiting for a change in my finances. I'm waiting for a change in my job. I'm waiting to be closer to God. I'm waiting for Christian growth. I'm waiting for my children to be delivered and receive Jesus as their Lord and Savior. I'm waiting for doors to open to my book ADDICTED. I'm even waiting to learn how to wait.

God you told me to write the book and you would open doors? I've written the book but when will the doors open? People say, "don't be surprised when you're on television." I know it will happen one day because of the witness in my spirit. I wish I knew when things will turn around in my life. When will you open me up like a flower in full bloom? When will you send me out into the world as your worker? When will I see the manifestation of your promises? You keep showing me things that are to come, and you tell me things too. How long must I wait for the good things to happen in my life? When will I have all that you have promised me? When will I have peace and prosperity? When will my children walk in the light of Christ? When will I live the blessed life? When will I have more than enough? I'm sure I'm not ready yet. You're still preparing me for that time. I know you're allowing me to spend time with my family. I feel like I won't see them much once you send me out. Thank you for the time with my family. I don't see them often enough but I'm still grateful.

I set my thoughts on faith projects, but I never stay in faith until the manifestation. I'm disappointed in myself for not waiting on God to move. He is teaching and molding me into the daughter He created. I'd say my life is moving in slow motion. But looking back over the past three years God has brought me a mighty long way. I'm thankful to be so special to God.

Help me Father to stay focused on you and only you. Bless those Father who judge or talk badly of me. Forgive those Father who say I love you too much. Help me Father to love everyone as Christ loves me. Help me Father not look at people for what they do. We wrestle not against flesh and blood. Most people think I'm just some lady who was addicted to drugs. They think my book is just some sordid story. Why can't they see what's really happening? It's a testimony about the goodness of God. You have told many the plans that you have for my life. I just thank you Father that I belong to you. I love you so much God and I thank you for loving me. I thank you for your patience with me. I never knew true, unconditional love until you showed me.

God is so faithful, and he has shown me that time and time again. I trust in him always. The world is in his hands and that's the best place to be. Until God tells me exactly what to do, I won't do anything. It's not easy knowing when to wait and when to move. I won't allow is the enemy to put me in condemnation. God already knows I will make mistakes. Nothing I do is a surprise to God. He created me and knows me better than I know myself.

Waiting on God important and how you wait is equally if not more important. Take for example my current job, from the moment I began it was like a whirlwind. It reminded me of a tornado. The winds were blowing and leaving destruction behind. I was spinning so fast and things were changing so fast that I could barely keep up. Before I got used to one thing, something else was already happening. I was so unhappy, angry and discouraged every day. I complained, grumbled, kicked and screamed the whole way. I couldn't quit because I was where God wanted me to be. I didn't understand because God does things decent and in order. I know He is not the author or confusion but there was confusion all around me. Then one day someone told me that God was training me. She said I needed to watch people and listen to them. I was reminded of the morning God woke me up and I saw a vision of a seal. I looked up the significance of a seal and it said I needed to say to listen for what people are not saying. She was saying the same thing. I shared this with another friend, and she reminded me that I become upset when things change. I went to God and repented for not doing his will and being rebellious. I asked God to renew my mind and create a right spirit within me. I stopped complaining and began to look at the circumstances differently. I don't want to waste time being angry and unproductive during this season. Instead I want to do everything and learn everything that God has sent me to do. I want to focus on hearing from God. I believe my character and endurance are being strengthened. I must reach my destiny in the time God has given me here. Praying more and spending time in the presence of God will bring me closer to him. I have become so comfortable in saying that I'm waiting on God. I'm not waiting on God because he already knows our end. He is the Alpha and the Omega and everything in between.

    I thought I was waiting on God, but He was with me the entire time. I was on the right path but instead of relaxing and embracing the season, I complained. I wanted to know the plan God has for me. I must stop trying to see the whole picture all at once. It's more than I can handle. I believe, it would be easier to break down into smaller parts.

    I wanted to know the end of my journey before I reached it. God continued to send help and guidance along the way. But I couldn't see it because I was focused on the end. I didn't know how to be content where I was. If I knew my end, I would probably never reach it. God is preparing me for the next season on my journey. I must be still so that I can grow, and God will change me. In the past, I was a quitter and a runner. Now God is teaching me to be still and know that he is God. I'm moving forward, and life keeps getting better as I draw nearer to God.

Waiting has severe side effects such as anxiety and fear. Waiting drains your strength and energy and renders you hopeless. That is if you complain the whole time. Waiting will steal your joy and leave an open portal for the enemy to enter in. Every day I learn something new from God. He shows me things He will connect for me later. If I lived to be one thousand years old, I still wouldn't know it all. Some days I start to feel like I don't know enough or I'm not good enough. Then God sends a word to remind me that His grace is sufficient. It is important to wait on God so that things continue to go smoothly. This will lessen the chance of confusion and offense. saying a word. It's true that what concerns me, concerns God. He watches out for his people. He works it out so that everyone is happy and safe.

I never know when or how God will use me, but I say "yes" to his will. I have a new role as vice president of education in my Toastmaster's club. I didn't want to do it, but I felt God wanted me to. I must receive God's grace and know that it is working in my life. I receive it by faith. I began operating in my new role, which is something that I've never done before. I know that I have the grace to be super successful in it. I will accomplish everything that God intends for me to accomplish while serving him. I realize that this is all for the glory of God. I started thinking about changes I would make. I want the group to grow in every way. Then I was reminded it's not my group, it belongs to God. He has a plan and a purpose for placing me in this position. I'm here because there's something He needs to get done. Through me His will shall be done, in Jesus name. I must remember to call on the Lord for everything I need. I must listen to his voice and obey his commands and instructions. I have a lot to do but if God is for me; who can be against me. I'll keep my eyes on God because he orders my steps.

    I continuously ask God to change me and help me to treat others with love. I'm not just saying it, but I mean it with all my heart. I have a burning desire to please God in all I do. God is answering my prayers and others are seeing it with their own eyes. I'll continue to testify about all that God is doing for me. My faith will continue to grow and so will the faith of those whose faith is weaker than mine.

Ephesians 6:16 tells me that above all, take the shield of faith with me which I will be able to quench all the fiery darts of the wicked one. So therefore, my actions while I wait are faith moves. My job is to keep my faith working until the fiery darts are extinguished. Sometimes a heaviness tries to settle on me as I wait on God. But the moment I realize its presence I hold up the shield of faith which is the word of God. My faith is in God and everything He says. I must walk, act and think like my prayers have already been answered. In doing so it means that I will not be constantly talking about the situation as I see it. I will confess the word of God out of my mouth. God says if I believe I've received it, then it's mine.

Every day I wake up expecting something to be different. But it always looks the same. I won't stop looking for God to turn it all around. While I wait, I will keep on doing what He tells me to do. I believe with all my heart that God is who He says he is. He'll do everything he says he will do. If only I could get it right. If only I knew the word of God and how to apply to my life. I must wait until He teaches me. It doesn't happen overnight although I wish it would. Then it wouldn't hurt so bad. I yearn to see a change in my life. I want to live the Kingdom life. I know there'll always be trouble but how long will I have to live in it. I never know how I'm going to make it, but I know I will. God is the head of my life. One of the first scriptures that was given to me was taken from Psalm 46, "be still and know that I am God." I must be still and in constant communication with God. I can't question whether it seems right or wrong to me. I can't wonder why He chose to do it this way. I trust him because he is God.

    I wait for God because I trust him. He is not a man that he should lie. Even though I am being pressed on every side, I won't be crushed. In fact, I already have the victory through Christ Jesus. I no longer question whether God will do it because I know he will. Instead I ask myself what's in my way slowing it down. What's obstructing God's promises from reaching me. The answer can likely be found in me. The abundant life belongs to me so what's the hinderance? I wrestle not against flesh and blood but against principalities. Greater is He that is in me than He that is in the world. I trust God totally because **Romans 8:28(KJV) says, and we know that all things work together for**

good to them that love God, to them who are the called according to his purpose. I wish I could see in the spirit realm right now. I know the angels are warring on my behalf.

    I was talking with someone the other day and he told me that he felt like quitting because he was tired of fighting. I encouraged him to keep fighting because he was so close to victory. It would be horrible to quit now. I could literally see him at the finish line as I encouraged him. Today I must encourage myself. The enemy wants me to think there is no way I will come out of this situation. But when I think about who God is, this is nothing for him. I'm waiting and at the same time I'm fighting. My faith is in the Word of God. I don't care what it looks like. I am not moved by how hopeless it looks because I've got a word from God. His word is alive, active and working in my life. I'll talk less and speak the word more.

    God already knows how I feel so why not say it anyway. I immediately tell him that I trust him. I trust God and I don't even trust myself. I must put one foot in front of the other and walk. I trust God because he knows the end from the beginning. He knows everything along my journey. He has already made a way of escape. I will seek him in all things. He will guide me to victory, and He will get the glory. That would please me more than anything. I won't deny that my flesh gets in the way sometimes. Sometimes cry and plead with God to make the pain go away. That is the pain that comes from the desires of the flesh. I realize I'm only here for God's purpose. He is the Ruler and Creator of all things. He is all powerful. I love him more than I love anything in the world. I'm not saying that I always do or say the right thing. I'm just saying I want to do what is right. I want to do what is pleasing to my Father. I want the light of Christ to shine so brightly through me that others will want the same. I ask God continuously to remove everything in me that's not like him. I ask him to make me more like him. I want to be a soul winner. If I don't lead people to the Lord, I want to impact their lives. I can never get enough of talking about God. I will live one day at time a time. I won't worry about tomorrow because it would be a burden on me.

    I'm waiting on God to do so many things in my life. If He would just renew my mind, I would be so grateful. I know that He's always working on my behalf. God says to cast your burdens on him but sometimes I take them back.

I pray and ask God questions. I also ask him to show me things about me and my life. I know there are things from my past that are affecting me now. I don't exactly know what they are, but God does. At just the right time He will reveal the truth to me. He is so faithful. I ask him to heal me of any brokenness and he'll do it. I keep moving and wait until He shows me the truth. Then the healing process can begin. But I must be patient and wait for God to guide me through each step. Sometimes it can be so painful that I want to rush through it. But God knows what's best for me.

I feel like God is waiting for me to do something, but I don't know what it is. I'm doing something wrong because God will always respond when I pray His will. I know God would never withhold any good thing from me. I know that the Lord loves me very much. I understand that God is not my servant. It is my faith that is assigned to serve me. God does not do magic, he performs miracles. He is my Father and he does not lie.

I must stop waiting on God because he's waiting for me. When God tells me to do something I often wait before I do it. Yet every time I ask Him to do something, I expect him to jump. He is not my servant; He is the Creator.

God has been giving me instructions for a long time. I all too often get distracted. I continue to pray and make petitions to God. He's waiting for me to complete the assignment he's already given me. I should always be doing something. I'm constantly asking God questions and asking him to do things for me. But most of the time my answers lie in my incomplete assignments.

I ask God for more wisdom, so I won't be so easily confused. Recently, it was time to have my license plates renewed on my car. I didn't have the money to purchase them. I confessed the word to him that He would supply all my needs. Every scripture that had to do with need and provision I quoted daily. I continued to give tithes and offerings. I could have easily taken the tithe and bought the plates for my car. But that would have been stealing from God. I knew I was doing the right thing because I owe that to God. I prayed and asked God why I never have the money I need? I'm always waiting until last minute and this time was no different. The day came and went and now my plates were past due. I had a dream that the police pulled me over for not using my turn signal. They gave me a ticket. At first, I thought this was a warning from God to be careful. But the dream couldn't have been from God. Everything from God is good and a ticket is not good. A part of me didn't understand why I was riding around on illegal plates. I know God can get money to me when I need it. He says that He shall supply all my needs. Since the law requires me to register my car every year it was a need. What was I doing wrong? Was this an area God was trying to grow and develop my faith? I wasn't exactly sure, but I do know that I trust God. He has shown me so many times that He is with me. God has helped me even when I didn't know I needed help. So surely, He wouldn't change now. The bible says in **Hebrews 13:8(NIV) *Jesus Christ is the same yesterday and today and forever.***

I had a book signing scheduled for two days after my plates expired. The book sales were amazing. I had never sold so many books before. At the end of the day I counted the money. I had enough to buy my license plates. I was very grateful for God's favor on that day. But then I started thinking and that's when I almost got into trouble again. It was Saturday and the banks were closed. I separated the money in two piles. One pile was to be deposited into my account. This way I could buy more books to sell. The other pile was to be put aside for my plates until God gave me the rest of the money. I would pray and ask God where I should sow a seed. I needed more money to pay for my plates. I was going to wait on God. I wanted him to tell me how to do what He had already done. This was insanity. Then God talked some sense into me. I realized that He had already answered my prayer. It was Him who had sent the people to buy the books. I used the money to pay for my license plates.

I must make God's instructions a priority in my life. Writing this book just happens to be one of them. He told me to write this book at least six months ago. I'm taking my sweet time and I don't even know how much time I have left. I must do the things God has told me to. Maybe then He would give me another assignment. Whoever can be trusted with very little can also be trusted with much. I am responsible to show God that He can trust me in little things. Perhaps when I complete the small things, he will move me to bigger things. The truth is that He's trying to help me and I'm not doing my part. I told God that I would do better because I want Him to trust me with more.

A lot of things that God has promised to do for me have been held up by bitterness and offense. I continue to ask God to forgive me and circumcise my heart. The feelings that are in the heart are real and only God can heal me. But he's waiting for me to really want it. God doesn't force us to do anything. I listen to my pastors and I listen to video teachings. One morning I was listening to a minister teaching about KEYS TO THE KINGDOM. He said the first key was forgiveness. He referenced the scriptures, **Matthew 5:23-24(NLT), "So if you are presenting a sacrifice at the altar in the Temple and you suddenly remember that someone has ought against you, 24 "leave your** *sacrifice there at the altar. Go and be reconciled to that person. Then come and offer your sacrifice to God."* I meditated on the message I heard. The Lord told me to call my mother and I did. Prior to this we hadn't talked in more than a month. I called her but she didn't answer the phone. I left her a very pleasant message. She called me back and I was glad she did. We talked for more than half an hour. I was glad to talk to her and I could tell that she was equally glad to talk with me. While I was waiting on God, He was waiting on me to let it all go. I had to forgive in order to grow. For this I'll never wait again because I want all that God has for me. I want to be closer to him and I never want anything separating me from God. Yesterday I could see chains breaking in the spirit. Oh, glory to God the Father. I realize I must stay on course. I will live life God's way and not mine. God is building my endurance so that I can run my race. I will finish it for his glory.

I went to visit my mom today. The visit went well until I got ready to leave. She said that it was good to see me and asked for a hug. As I hugged her, she said she thought our relationship may change because I'd moved out. The devil reminded me that we didn't have a relationship before I moved in. Although the enemy wanted me to repeat those words, I did not. I must continue to think positive no matter what. I must cast down every negative thought as soon as it comes. I choose not to be offended another day and to walk in perfect love. I choose to be the bigger person every time. I will not grow weary in well doing. I will keep moving forward in victory.

I am determined to change my ways and be completely obedient to God's commands. When I know God tells me to do something and I don't do it, I'm wasting time. Living life for God is anything but boring.

God gave me a vision of a driving school. This school trains CDL drivers. I was waiting for God to tell me what to do but He already had. So finally, I went to the school. I went inside and sat down and talked with the very nice lady at the desk. As it turned out she is a woman of faith. I told her why I came and that I didn't know what to do next. We both agreed that God would show me what to do next. This school costs a lot of money that I didn't currently have. But that doesn't matter when it comes to God. He always shows up in my life and He's always right on time. I know that my faith is growing because I feel different inside. When things are happening around me, my reactions are different. Everything inside of me seems to be settled and undisturbed. I don't have a desire to drive a school bus or even a semi-truck. But I'll do anything God wants me to do. Because I love God, my answer to him is yes. I'm waiting until He leads me where I need to be.

I'm beginning to realize that God never really makes me wait. He's already provided everything I need. He's already given me the provision and the instructions I'll need to keep moving forward. I can see the goodness of the Lord. God created us all for greatness. When we received Jesus Christ as our Lord and Savior, the Greater One lives inside us.

It seems like I have so much to do. The truth is some of it should have already been done. But I can do all things through Christ who gives me strength. I'll keep going full speed ahead. I'm pressing forward toward the mark. I'm not confused about staying in communication with God. I take nothing for granted no matter how good it sounds. I must consult God on all things concerning me. It's not my life that I'm living, I belong to the Lord. I'm here for His purpose only. I have no prior training for all that God is calling me to do. But I am in training even now. In addition to that, I have God's unmerited favor.

I've wasted so much time waiting for God. I should have been asking God to show me what was wrong with me. I should have known the delay had something to do with me. God is my Father and wants me to have access to everything He promised. But just like my earthly father; why would God reward me for doing wrong? Rewards are given for doing what's right. God told me to love my neighbor as myself. I'm always upset and feuding with my neighbor; why would He reward me? He couldn't even if He wanted to because of my actions. The only thing that stops God from moving in my life is me.

I'm working on changing the things I do. I don't know why I'm this way, but with God all things are possible. God will change me, and He will clean me up on the inside. He will make all things new. God has brought me such a long way and yet I have so far to go. The good thing is that I'm willing to let him change me. Make me more like you God. Yes, I want all your promises to manifest in my life. I want you to be pleased with me in every way. Lord teach me to walk in perfect love with you.

As soon as I have a made-up mind to focus on what God has told me to do. Here come the distractions. The fiery darts are constantly being thrown at me. No weapon formed against me shall prosper, in Jesus name. Yet in all these things, I am more than a conqueror. God has provided everything I will ever need. He created flowers, plants and animals and he will provide for me. How much more valuable am I than a plant to God? I'm reminded of a certain day when my dad was alive. We were sitting outside, and bees swarmed everywhere. Everyone was running and swatting the bees trying not to be stung. My dad was sitting at the picnic table with his legs crossed. Several bees swarmed around his head. He never moved and he didn't stop talking. As I ran past him, I asked how he could sit there surrounded by bees? He stated, "I won't bother them, and they won't bother me." Never did I imagine how significant that day would be in my life. I must look at the fiery darts and distractions the same way, as if there're not even there. The bible says in **Luke 10:19, (KJV) "Behold, I give unto you power to tread on serpents and scorpions, and over all the power of the enemy: and nothing shall by any means hurt you."** They cannot harm me unless I submit to them. I must continue to walk right through the darts and distractions. The blood of Jesus covers me. I take with me the shield of faith, the breastplate of righteousness and the sword of the spirit.   I will keep serving God and doing His will. If God be for me, who can be against me.

It appears much of my waiting deals with money and finances. But how can I be waiting for things that God has already provided for me. So many bills are due, and I can't imagine how they will be paid. Lord show me which way to go. I owe out more money than I am bringing in. It becomes so overwhelming sometimes and then I pray. I pray for peace and provision. Nothing is more important than knowing the word of God.

Because until I do, it won't work in my life. I know I will not lose anything that belongs to me because that is not God's will. Everything that I have, He gave to me. The scripture says in **3 John 1:2(NKJV) "Beloved, I pray that you may prosper in all things and be in health, just as your soul prospers."**

I was listening to sermon today by a pastor and he said when God fed the children of Israel with manna. They were not allowed to keep any for the next day. This was a revelation to me that I should not worry about tomorrow and it even says so in bible. **Matthew 6:34(NIV) "Therefore do not worry about tomorrow, for tomorrow will worry about itself. Each day has enough trouble of its own**." Worrying is a distraction and it is not from God, so I won't worry. I have plenty to do so that I don't have to wait. I should be digging into the word and finding ways to make it happen. **Psalm 119:105, "Thy word is a lamp unto my feet, and a light unto my path."** God has already done all He is going to do and so he rested on the seventh day. Waiting is not an option because Jesus said, "it is finished." He's finished and it's my turn to do my part.

I had a seed that I wanted to sow because I need to reap a harvest. I prayed and asked God where I could sow my seed. A day or two later, he led me to a place, where I sowed the seed into someone. Then I sowed another seed because I was reminded of the scripture that says in **2 Corinthians 9:6(KJV) "But this I say, He which soweth sparingly shall reap also sparingly; and he which soweth bountifully shall reap also bountifully."** I sowed bountifully and I knew I would see a harvest very soon. Within 24 hours the enemy was trying to steal my harvest. He began telling me that my seed would not produce because I had not sown into good soil. The devil is a liar and I began to command my harvest to come in. Not only did I sow money, but I sowed in food too. It didn't stop there because I sowed seeds of encouragement and prayer. I shall reap a hundred-fold harvest. I thank God that Jesus rebuked the devourer for my sake, and he shall not destroy the fruits of my ground.

I continue to wait on God and many changes are taking place in my life. I would say that God's timing is perfect. I never want to wait for answers or solutions. I want it all right now. But if He gave it to me now, I couldn't even handle it. I would probably be overwhelmed if I knew everything that God knows. His way is perfect, and my way is pitiful. He knows when I'm ready to hear the truth and except it. I must be able to see it before I can be cleansed and restored. It's a journey and the roads are often bumpy along the way. I even encounter potholes every now and then. I've got to keep moving if I want to grow and be cleansed. I used to be too stubborn to move. I stood still waiting for something to happen. God said that his people are destroyed for lack of knowledge. I try to read the bible, study, meditate and listen to the word of God. I will not perish. God gives me instructions where to go and what to do next. He places new people in my life and new assignments. I've learned not to get upset when things change. God is indeed the boss and may change things for my good. I pray daily and listen for God to speak to me. Some days He speaks and sometimes he doesn't. It's disappointing when I don't hear him. I would love to talk with him every day. But He is faithful, and I will hear him when He has something to say. I want to quickly carry out his instructions when they come. This way I will be ready when God speaks again. It's satisfying to my spirit to complete an instruction from God.

I believe everything God shows me will happen. I'm using everything I've been taught to stand in adversity. ***2 Corinthians 10:5 (NLT) says, "We destroy every proud obstacle that keeps people from knowing God. We capture their rebellious thoughts and teach them to obey Christ."*** This is spiritual warfare. The enemy is trying to keep me from receiving what God has for me. I will have everything that God has for me, in Jesus name. ***Ephesians 3:20 (NKJV), "Now to Him who is able to do exceedingly abundantly above all that we ask or think, according to the power that works in us."*** God promises me in Malachi that because I am a tither, He will rebuke the devourer for my sakes, So, that he will not destroy the fruit of my ground.

Many people are content with not going to church but there's a word going forth in the house of the Lord. There the body of Christ is interceding on your behalf so don't stay home and fight alone. Sometimes the enemy tries to wear me down to exhaustion. God has warriors interceding on my behalf.

   Sometimes I look at my present situation and it looks sad. But I've learned not to look so far ahead. I'll just take one day at a time. I see how God is taking care of me. When I look at my life one day at a time, I realize I have all I need.

HE'S WAITING FOR ME

I'll keep trusting God and looking for things He has shown me. Sometimes the enemy makes me question whether I really have faith. But in my heart, I know I do. I have discovered that I cannot wait and do nothing. When I do nothing, my faith does nothing. I believe waiting is a trick of the enemy. While it is true that we must wait on God, there is more to it than that. God shows us things that belong to us and the devil tries to steal them away. The enemy tries to prevent us from receiving all the wonderful things God has for us. **John 10:10 (NIV) says "The thief comes only to steal and kill and destroy; I have come that they may have life and have it to the full."** I must start thinking and acting like it's already mine. I moved my faith from what God had already shown me. The enemy thought he was so cunning but I'm not having it. Thanks be to God who leads me in all things. My faith must be active and working to bring in the promises of God. If I don't keep it active it's not working, and it loses power. My faith will produce the promises of God in my life in Jesus name. I'll keep confessing, speaking and believing what God says and shows me. I will not be anxious while I wait. I will not be deceived by the enemy. I will stay in communication with God who orders my step.

Praise God for showing me that it's not him who should be performing. It's me who must perform. God has already done everything He needs to do. He created Adam and provided everything he would need. Then He placed him in the garden. He is the same God and he did the same for us. Yes, we must study his word and know his will for our lives. If we don't the enemy can tell us anything and we'll believe it.

We can be so close to the blessings of God and miss it by listening to the lies of the devil. I won't miss it because I know the plans God has for my life. While I am waiting, God is reminding me that I'm not alone. I recently received a phone call from a friend who is seeking God for direction. He says that he is not hearing from God and doesn't know what to do. I prayed with him and encouraged him to trust God and wait for the

Lord. I also told him to read the word of God. God speaks through his Word. I've encouraged him now I must encourage myself in the Lord. I must dig into the Word with both feet, heels and all my toes. God says that he'll never leave me nor forsake me.

I heard the Lord say the word "strategy" to me today. I only wish I knew what he meant by it. I prayed and asked him to give me understanding. No good thing will he hold from them who walk uprightly. The devil starts trying to steal it my faith in what God says. He can't steal the word of God, so he is trying to steal my faith. God can't give me what I don't believe in. I recently started to understand the way the enemy works. I must always consult God and believe. I know that I'm still a target for the enemy. He is nothing more than a thief and a liar.

For a while, I waited for God as if something was going to drop out of the sky. But nothing happened. I tried to figure out what I was doing wrong. In the process the enemy was trying to ruin my life. God sent people to tell me I didn't know the Word. Yet I continued to be lazy and disobedient. I should have made it priority to study the Word. But I allowed every distraction to keep me from it. God was telling me what to do and I still didn't do it. I continued to look to him for answers that he had already given me. God wasn't ignoring me; I was ignoring his instructions. I guess it wasn't the answer that I was looking for. I kept asking the same question over and over. God is so merciful. I was looking for the answer I wanted to hear. I was trying to do it my way instead of God's way. That was a huge waste of time. My disobedience caused frustration and confusion. It opened the door for the enemy to come in. He began to remind me of my past. He told me I didn't deserve the promises of God and I never would. Listening to this made me so sad because I love the Lord so much. I started to believe there was a limit to what I could have from God. I was convinced that I didn't deserve anything big from God. I thought I was being punished because of my past. The devil is a liar. I would never have known this without reading the Word.

God is trying to get something done in the earth. He created me to do something for him.

His plans didn't change because I missed some things along the way. His will shall be done. Not by power, nor by might but from the pouring out of His Spirit. There is no condemnation for them who are in Christ Jesus. I must run this race and run it fast because there isn't much time left. Things are changing and the atmosphere is shifting. I see things that I've never seen before. In all this, I still thank God that I'm not where I used to be. I thank Him for being so patient with me and loving me. Despite the things I do, He continues to bless me.

    I continue to seek God. It does matters how I wait. So, I wait with thanksgiving in my heart. God loves me and He is faithful. I know good things are ahead of me. I trust God because he says, "When the enemy shall come in like a flood, the Spirit of the LORD shall lift up a standard against him. My God shall supply all my needs, according to his riches in glory by Christ Jesus, in Jesus name. I'll spend the rest of the day thanking God just because He is God and worthy of it all.

My hope for you is that after reading this book you will gain some insight and peace about your journey. I pray that you will not spend as much time waiting as you do studying the will and ways of God. Then you will understand the power that you have through Christ Jesus. When and if you find yourself waiting for something to happen that you prayed for, go back to God and ask him for the truth. Ask him where your prayer is in the spirit realm. Ask him if you have done all you need to do. Ask him is there something inside you that's hindering your prayers. It may be unforgiveness.   Keep seeking him until you receive an answer, or your prayer is manifested. Remember timing counts too. God's timing that is and not ours. Most importantly always trust God through the process because he wants what's best for us.

www.ingramcontent.com/pod-product-compliance
Lightning Source LLC
Chambersburg PA
CBHW031634160426

43196CB00006B/416